200 years of the Monmouthshire the Brecknock & Abergavenny Canal an illustrated history

CONTENTS

1759

The first canal

The first of Britain's inland canals was born of the desire of Francis Egerton, 3rd Duke of Bridgewater, to transport vast quantities of coal from his mines at Worsley to the rapidly expanding industrial town of Manchester. The only forms of transport at this time were the costly and slow horse and cart or packhorse.

James Brindley was employed to design and engineer this radical project and the Bridgewater Canal opened in 1761, replacing packhorses with new horse-drawn narrowboats.

The economics of scale were obvious as one packhorse carried only two hundredweight of goods (90kg), whereas one of the Duke's horse-drawn narrowboats carried approximately 20 tons, equating to 200 horses. This ensured the rapid development of this new form of transportation. 'Canal mania' had arrived.

1792

Canals planned for the Usk Valley

In the 18th Century the valleys of South Wales were blessed with a wealth of iron ore, limestone, timber and coal. Easy access to a plentiful supply of water ensured that small-scale industries sprang up in the valleys to exploit these raw materials. Charcoal burning, iron smelting and lime manufacture all became commonplace.

However, the geographical isolation of these industries meant that heavy goods were difficult, expensive and slow to transport via packhorse. With the industrial revolution underway demand for these raw materials was rapidly growing.

The valleys required better transport links and in 1792 the Monmouthshire Canal was conceived by a group of wealthy businessmen, notably Josiah Wedgewood (potter), Henry Somerset (5th Duke of Beaufort) and Thomas Hill (ironmaster). They submitted their scheme to Parliament and secured an Act authorising the construction of the canal and establishing the shareholders as the Company of Proprietors of the Monmouthshire Canal Navigation. The canal was planned to run from Pontnewynydd (north of Pontypool) to the river Usk at Newport and included an arm to Crumlin along the Ebbw Valley. Its primary purpose was transportation of coal and iron to the docks at Newport.

During this period the Brecknock & Abergavenny Canal was also conceived, again by a group of businessmen, some of whom were shareholders in the Monmouthshire Canal (most notably the 5th Duke of Beaufort). Through another Act of Parliament the Company of Proprietors of the Brecknock & Abergavenny Canal Navigation was formed. It differed from the Monmouthshire in that its initial purpose was simply to lower the transportation costs of coal, lime and farm produce between local markets.

The planning phase

1792

Surveying commences

In 1792 surveying the Usk Valley was undertaken by Thomas Dadford Jnr and his brother John, assisted by their father Thomas Snr who had worked with James Brindley on the Staffordshire & Worcestershire Canal.

The Monmouthshire Canal was surveyed first and found to require 42 locks to raise it 447ft in its 11 mile length from Newport to Pontnewynydd; the 11 mile arm to Crumlin required a further 32 locks to raise the canal about 365ft. Then the Brecknock & Abergavenny Canal (B&A) was surveyed and this required only six locks in the 33 miles from Pontymoile to Brecon. Remarkably, Dadford planned the canal to run for 23 miles from Pontymoile to Llangynidr uninterrupted at 367ft above sea level. The canal was to be cut into a shelf following the hilly terrain on the south side of the Usk Valley, before rising in six locks to 427ft, terminating at Brecon.

Initially, there was no plan to join the two canals as the B&A was originally to have its own connection with the river Usk at Newbridge. However, it was not long before the Monmouthshire Canal Company (MCC) saw both the financial benefits and security in water supply of linking their canal to the proposed B&A. The added benefit to the B&A was the saving in cost of locking all the way down to the river Usk. MCC agreed to pay the B&A £3,000 and honour the proposed B&A tolls if the route was changed to join the Monmouthshire Canal at Pontymoile; this was accepted and the routes revised.

Dadford designed the Brecknock & Abergavenny Canal in conjunction with three main tramroads: Beaufort to Gilwern, Gilwern to Glangrwyney and Llanfoist to Abergavenny. Acts of Parliament were passed (1792 for the Monmouthshire Canal, 1793 for the Brecknock & Abergavenny Canal) to allow the land to be compulsorily purchased and works to commence. These acts listed all major share owners, specified tolls and how the share capital was structured.

Since these canals would be isolated Dadford did not have to design the locks to conform to the traditional 6ft 10in by 72ft narrowboats, but choose to copy the design he'd adopted in the building of the Glamorganshire Canal a few years earlier, whose locks were around 65ft long and 9ft 6in wide.

1794

Construction begins on the Monmouthshire Canal

Digging of the canal channel was very labour intensive, employing vast numbers of men with picks, horses and barrows. The term "navigators" was given to these workers because they were building a "navigation"; by the 1830s this term had been shortened to "navvies".

Bridges, of local stone, were assembled using wooden formers on which stone arches were built.

The canal was divided into sections whose construction was often awarded to local tradesmen. Overnight, former shopkeepers and farmers become "canal cutters".

Progress was rapid, and in 1796 the main line of the Monmouthshire Canal opened between Pontnewynydd and Newport.

1796

Construction begins on the Brecknock & Abergavenny Canal

Work started in Penpedairheol, two miles west of Gilwern, digging both forward towards Llangynidr and back towards the site of the proposed embankment at Gilwern. This was one of the largest engineering feats of the entire project as the canal had to cross the Clydach Gorge over 90ft below.

Initially the River Clydach and the existing Clydach Rail Road had to be bridged in preparation for the construction of the embankment which carried the canal. The Clydach Rail Road was built by the Brecknock & Abergavenny Canal Company and engineered by John Dadford in 1794. By 1797 the canal had reached Llangynidr and the first lock had been constructed.

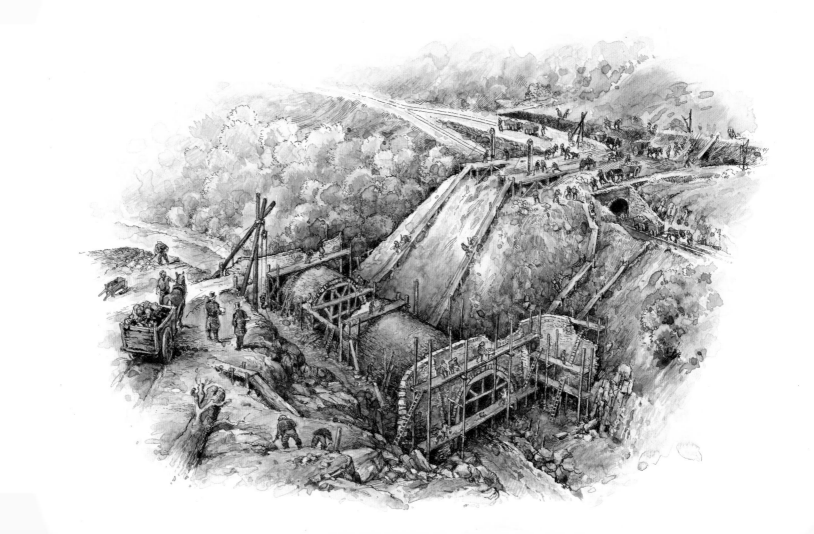

Dadford's sophisticated surveying allowed the majority of height to be gained between Newport and Pontymoile, from where the canal continued on one level to Llangynidr. Here five locks were constructed: two singles and a flight of three, with one side pond for water storage.

The majority of the water for the locks and the canal came from the river Usk, half a mile upstream of the canal terminus in Brecon. A weir was constructed on the river and a culvert to link this to the canal was built under the town. A small amount of water came from streams, known as "feeders".

By the end of 1799 the canal had reached Talybont on Usk via the five locks and a 375 yard tunnel, which became known as the Ashford tunnel.

1799

Completion of the Crumlin Arm

1799 also saw the completion of the Crumlin Arm which climbed 32 locks to about 365ft above sea level in its 11 miles; 38 boats were reportedly trading on this stretch within the year.

The Cefn Flight of fourteen locks at Rogerstone was one of Thomas Dadford Jnr's greatest engineering achievements and is now designated an Ancient Monument. For further in-depth information visit the Fourteen Locks Centre, built at the top end of the flight.

The lock flight rose 168ft within half a mile. Balance ponds and pounds were built to assist water flow and conservation.

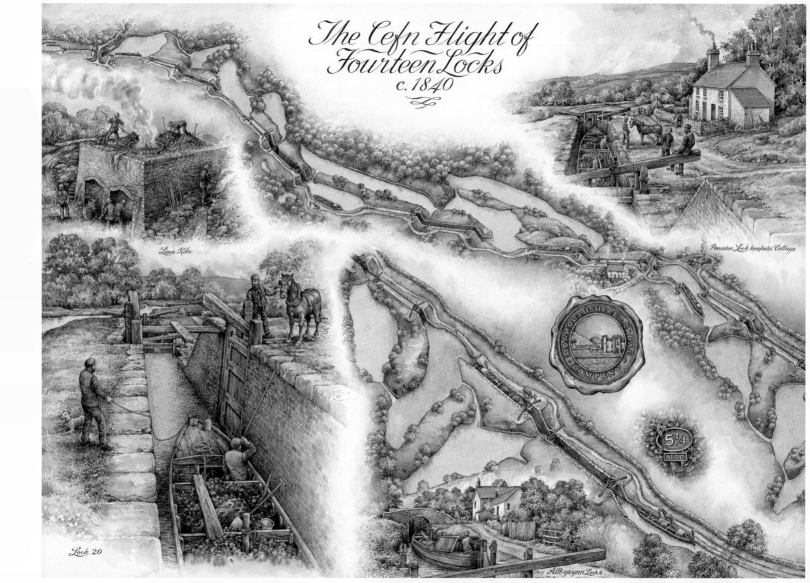

The Cefn Flight of
Fourteen Locks
c.1840

Lime Kiln

Pensarn Lock keepers Cottage

Lock 20

MONMOUTHSHIRE CANAL COMPANY

5¼
MCC

Allt-yr-ynn Lock 6

Thomas Dadford's four-arched stone aqueduct across the river Usk at Brynich opened in 1800.

The aqueduct was constructed using Brindley's method of making wooden formers – similar to bridge construction – over which stone arches were built; it towered 25ft above the river Usk.

By the end of 1800 the Brecknock & Abergavenny Canal was declared open from Gilwern to Brecon.

1812

The two canals merge at Pontymoile

The merger had been planned much earlier but the construction of the Brecknock & Abergavenny Canal suffered many setbacks, including the death of Thomas Dadford Jnr in 1801 at the age of 40. He was succeeded as engineer by Thomas Cartwright, who discovered that funding had been exhausted. In 1804 a further Act was submitted to Parliament for approval for additional funding; it took until 1805 for the canal to reach Govilon.

The Monmouthshire Canal Company had by now lost patience and was taking legal advice on seeking compensation from the Brecknock & Abergavenny Canal Company for loss of income.

In 1809, eager for his iron to reach Newport more competitively, Richard Crawshay, a Merthyr Tydfil ironmaster, invested £30,000 to complete the canal from Govilon to Pontymoile.

A year later, under the supervision of William Crosley, former engineer on the Rochdale Canal, work commenced on sections between Govilon and Pontymoile.

By February 1812 the connection was complete forming a 44 mile canal from Newport Docks to Brecon rising 427ft through 37 locks (31 on the Monmouthshire Canal and 6 on the Brecknock & Abergavenny Canal).

The Monmouthshire Canal Company had waited 18 years to see a return on their initial £3000 investment.

Construction of the canals enabled previously isolated industries to have access to both local and export markets through the port of Newport. Access to the canals was therefore vital, and a network of tramroads was constructed connecting various industrial sites to the canal. Where these tramroads met the canal, wharfs were built to trans-ship goods.

There were at least 14 tramroads connecting to the Monmouthshire Canal and 10 to the Brecknock & Abergavenny Canal covering many more miles than the two canals.

Stipulated in the two Parliamentary Acts was an agreement that tramroads originating from the canal and up to eight miles in length could be built without further permissions, provided that the tracks were open to all independent carriers. Carriers then paid tolls to owners of the tramroad dependent on weight and type of goods carried.

The term "tramroad" is used today for rails which had an 'L' shaped plate rail or tram plate; the tram wheels were plain and un-flanged. The alternative is for flanged wheels to run on edge rails known as railroads or railways. During the 18th and 19th centuries the terms were not well defined and it was common for both terms to describe the same rails. Tramroads of both types were in use on the Monmouthshire and Brecknock & Abergavenny Canals.

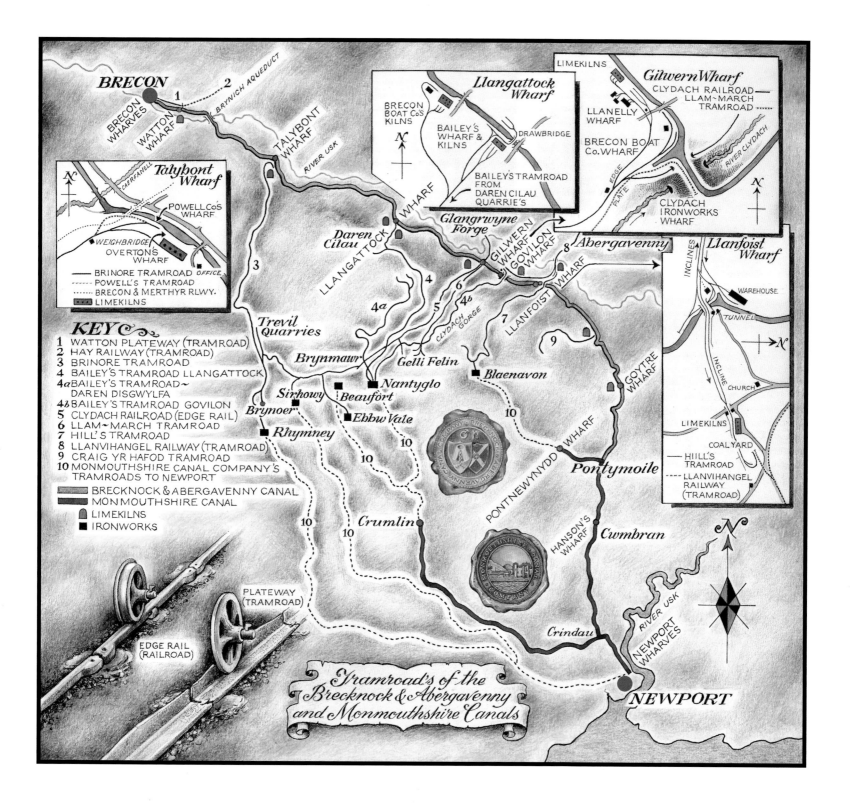

BRECON

BRECON WHARVES

WATTON WHARF

BRYNICH AQUEDUCT

2

1

TALYBONT WHARF

RIVER USK

Talybont Wharf

CAERFANELL

N

POWELL Co'S WHARF

WEIGHBRIDGE

OVERTON'S WHARF

OFFICE

— BRINORE TRAMROAD
···· POWELL'S TRAMROAD
---- BRECON & MERTHYR RLWY.
▦▦ LIMEKILNS

3

Daren Cilau

LLANGATTOCK WHARF

Llangattock Wharf

BRECON BOAT Co'S KILNS

BAILEY'S WHARF & KILNS

N

DRAWBRIDGE

BAILEY'S TRAMROAD FROM DAREN CILAU QUARRIE'S

LIMEKILNS

Gilwern Wharf

CLYDACH RAILROAD
LLAM~MARCH TRAMROAD ····

LLANELLY WHARF

BRECON BOAT Co. WHARF

RIVER CLYDACH

EDGE
PLATE

CLYDACH IRONWORKS WHARF

N

Glangrwyne Forge

GILWERN WHARF

GOVILON WHARF

8

Abergavenny

LLANFOIST WHARF

4

6

4b

5

CLYDACH GORGE

7

9

Llanfoist Wharf

INCLINES

WAREHOUSE

TUNNEL

N

INCLINE

INCLINE

CHURCH

LIMEKILNS

COALYARD

— HILL'S TRAMROAD
---- LLANVIHANGEL RAILWAY (TRAMROAD)

GOYTRE WHARF

Trevil Quarries

4a

Brynmawr

Gelli Felin

Blaenavon

KEY
1 WATTON PLATEWAY (TRAMROAD)
2 HAY RAILWAY (TRAMROAD)
3 BRINORE TRAMROAD
4 BAILEY'S TRAMROAD LLANGATTOCK
4a BAILEY'S TRAMROAD~ DAREN DISGWYLFA
4b BAILEY'S TRAMROAD GOVILON
5 CLYDACH RAILROAD (EDGE RAIL)
6 LLAM~MARCH TRAMROAD
7 HILL'S TRAMROAD
8 LLANVIHANGEL RAILWAY (TRAMROAD)
9 CRAIG YR HAFOD TRAMROAD
10 MONMOUTHSHIRE CANAL COMPANY'S TRAMROADS TO NEWPORT

▬▬ BRECKNOCK & ABERGAVENNY CANAL
▬▬ MONMOUTHSHIRE CANAL
▦ LIMEKILNS
■ IRONWORKS

Sirhowy

Beaufort

Nantyglo

Brynoer

Ebbw Vale

Rhymney

10

10

10

10

10

CANAL COMPANY · BRECKNOCK
ABERGAVENNY

MONMOUTHSHIRE CANAL COMPANY

PONTNEWYNYDD WHARF

Pontymoile

HANSON'S WHARF

Cwmbran

Crumlin

PLATEWAY (TRAMROAD)

EDGE RAIL (RAILROAD)

Crindau

RIVER USK

NEWPORT WHARVES

N

NEWPORT

Tramroad's of the Brecknock & Abergavenny and Monmouthshire Canals

c1850

Newport Docks

The link to the sea at Newport was vital to the commercial success of the canals and tramroads. At Newport Docks goods from the canal were transferred to ships destined for both local (mainly Bristol and Bridgewater in Somerset) and worldwide markets.

Iron ore in the Welsh hills was plentiful but of poor quality. In time imports of Spanish and Swedish ores of considerably higher grade were shipped through these docks destined mainly for the Blaenafon and Nantyglo Iron Works.

Situated at Two Locks, Cwmbran, this wharf was built by Cyrus Hanson for the manufacture of bricks and was in full production between 1853 and 1890.

The production technique used "fire clay" and coal brought down by the Henllys Tram Road. Hard white bricks were manufactured for use in kilns and furnaces.

c1850

Goytre Wharf

Lime kilns were constructed at numerous sites along the Brecknock & Abergavenny Canal, indicating its universal importance. The principal uses of lime were in agriculture as a fertilizer, and in the construction industry for both whitewash and building mortar (a mixture of lime and sand).

Lime was manufactured at Goytre Wharf between 1812 and approximately 1850.

Limestone was discharged into the top of the kilns and layered with coal. A fire was lit at the bottom creating a fierce heat (over 1000 ºC) which broke down the limestone to quick lime (a soluble powder) under a chemical reaction known as calcining. Eight to twelve hours later the hot lime was dug out from the draw arches in the base of the kiln and loaded into barrels to keep it dry for shipment.

By the 1860s many lime kilns had closed due to the invention of steam powered crushers, which powdered the limestone.

Machine Cottage (on the left of the picture) was built in 1812 to house the toll collector and weighing machine operator. Also housed were the mechanical levers and associated measuring weights for the weighing machine outside.

Wharfinger's Cottage and Hill's Warehouse were built between 1817 and 1818.

By 1820 construction of Hill's tramroad, from Blaenafon around Blorenge Mountain, via Garnddyrys Forge then down three inclined planes to Llanfoist Wharf, was complete. Its main purpose was to take advantage of the more competitive tolls offered on the Brecknock & Abergavenny Canal.

The wharf loaded pig iron from Hill's Blaenafon Iron Works, established in 1789, onto barges destined for Newport Docks. Spanish iron ore for use at the works was unloaded at the wharf and taken back up the incline.

The Wharfinger's Cottage housed the wharf manager and the pay office.

c1850

Llanfoist Wharf

Hill's tramroad continued down a fourth incline, via the cast iron canal bridge, into Llanfoist where coal and lime were trans-shipped to the Llanvihangel Tramroad. This tramroad originating at Govilon Wharf was built by William Crosley between 1811 and 1829 and ran to Llanvihangel Crucorney. It was later extended to Hereford.

Limestone and coal were also brought down the incline to the kilns on what is now known as Kiln Lane.

The wharf at Govilon enabled trans-shipment from Bailey's Tramroad to the canal and the Llanfihangel Tramroad.

Bailey's tramroad was built between 1819 and 1821 and ran from Nantyglo Ironworks down the Clydach Gorge, carrying pig iron and coal to the canal.

It wasn't unknown for cattle and sheep to be transported by boats to markets along the canal. Locals sometimes used the canal to carry their furniture when moving house.

In the latter half of the 1800s when the Merthyr, Tredegar and Abergavenny Railway crossed the canal at Govilon a branch line was added to unload coal from the train to boats destined for Llangynidr. This activity did not cease until the early 1930s.

c1850

Gilwern Wharf

Three canal wharfs were built at Gilwern. The first of these was the Brecknock & Abergavenny Canal Company's Clydach Railroad Wharf constructed to trans-ship goods from the Clydach Railroad. The railroad was engineered by John Dadford, brother of Thomas, prior to works starting on the canal in 1794.

Limestone and iron ore carried on the Clydach Railroad also continued under the canal to Llangrwyney Forge situated alongside the river Usk. It was sited here to use water from the river to drive a water wheel powering the forge hammers.

Gilwern Wharf

The second wharf at Gilwern, known as Llanelly Wharf, belonged to the Brecknock Boat Company and was established for transportation of coal from Wain Dew colliery, near Brynmawr, onto boats destined for Brecon.

The third wharf was the Clydach Iron Company's Wharf which trans-shipped from the Llam-march Tramroad. This tramroad, built between 1793 and 1803, connected Clydach ironworks with the coalmines and iron ore deposits at Gellifelen and Llam-march and the canal at Gilwern.

c1850

Llangattock Wharf

Llangattock had three wharfs and two sets of lime kilns. The larger kilns and wharf were built in 1815 and leased by the Brecknock & Abergavenny Canal Company to the Brecknock Boat Company along with the tramroad that brought down limestone from the Llangattock Escarpment. In 1821 the Wharfinger's house nearby was built and leased to the Brecknock Boat Company.

The smaller kiln was built c1830 for J. & C. Bailey who also used the tramroad to bring down limestone and coal. Bailey built two additional inclines to link the tramroad to his Nantyglo Ironworks.

Opposite Bailey's kilns was their coal wharf, reached via a branch off the tramroad which crossed an iron drawbridge. From this wharf coal was trans-shipped to Brecon and local markets. This lime kiln was one of the last to be in use and only ceased operation in the 1920s.

c1850

Talybont on Usk Wharf

Benjamin Hall's Wharf at Talybont on Usk was the terminus of the Brinore Tramroad, in use between 1815 and 1864. It connected the canal to various collieries and quarries in the Rhymney area and was later connected to Hall's Rhymney Ironworks.

At just over 8 miles long this was one of the longest tramroads in the region. It was constructed with the locally adopted gauge of 3ft 4in, running on 'L' shaped rails held together by tie bars supported on stone block sleepers. Limestone, coal and iron were brought down from the South Wales valleys and pit props taken on the return journey for use in the mines.

c1850

Brecon Wharf

The main wharf at Brecon was the Brecknock & Abergavenny Canal Company's Watton Wharf. This served both the Watton Lime Kilns and the Hay Tramroad.

The wharf loaded coal, lime and limestone onto the Hay Tramroad which opened in 1816 connecting Brecon to Hay on Wye. In 1860 the tramroad was closed, and many lengths converted to rail, enabling steam trains to reach Brecon in 1863.

Brecon was a thriving market town with regular deliveries of timber, barrels of beer and farm produce unloading at one of the seven other wharfs: including the Brecknock & Abergavenny Canal Company, Hugh Bold and Brecknock Boat Company.

Packet boats from Newport brought goods from Bristol and around the world.

locks. Each lock consumed 40,000 gallons of water, lifting a boat approximately 9ft 6in.

Locks planned for the canal were designed with double bottom gates with integral paddles (which let the water out of the lock, like a bath plug), a single top gate with ground paddles either side water into the lock, like taps). Foot bridges were built at the bottom gates enabling boatmen to operate the paddles on each side.

Lock chambers were 65ft long and 9ft 6in wide and were built using local stone.

c1850

Ashford Tunnel northern entrance

In the construction of canals, tunnels were used where cuttings would be either too costly or too dangerous. There were only two locations that required tunnels: the first was just south of Sebastopol on the Monmouthshire Canal and the second just south of Talybont on Usk on the Brecknock & Abergavenny Canal.

The landscape at the proposed site of the Ashford tunnel dropped steeply to the river bed. The engineering solutions available were to continue cutting along the contour - shoring up the embankment from the river, or to tunnel through the slope. Tunnelling was considered to be the most cost effective option and work began from the southern end.

Construction of the Ashford Tunnel was not straight-forward and many problems were encountered, with a substantial portion of the tunnel collapsing during initial work. This collapse probably led to the remaining length being constructed by "cut and cover", the ground being excavated, the tunnel arch built and the earth replaced to reform the original landscape.

The width of the tunnel was 12ft, not wide enough for a boat and tow path. Boats, it is believed, were "legged" through the tunnel while the horse had to be taken along the towpath which continued above the tunnel.

Known as the Ashford Tunnel, it derives its name from a large country residence just to the north of the tunnel.

c1850

Brynich Aqueduct

Working boats on the canal were of wooden construction, pointed at both ends and measured around 9ft by 63ft. As trips were short, most boats were designed to have only day cabins.

The only non-wooden commercial boats on the canal were the iron ice breakers. These were rocked from side to side by a gang of men while being pulled by several horses.

On the Brecknock & Abergavenny Canal, transportation of coal peaked at around 37,000 tons per year in 1818/19; a yearly total of approximately 1,600 boat loads, an average of four boat trips each day. Limestone/lime transportation peaked at about 25,000 tons in the same period; an annual total of approximately 1,100 boat loads giving an average of over three trips every day.

The peak in transportation of iron on the canal came much later, in 1853/4 when approximately 75,000 tons per year were moved requiring 3,300 boat trips, an average of nine every day. The late peak of iron transportation arose from the demands of the development of railway construction from the 1840s onwards. Ironically the canal played a vital role in its own demise. Naturally, carriage of iron by canal had declined rapidly by the second half of the 1850s.

c1850

Talybont on Usk rail crossing

An Act of Parliament in 1848 enabled the Monmouthshire Canal Company to be renamed the Monmouthshire Railway and Canal Company thus showing the new importance of railways within the company.

In 1853, due to the lack of water, the company closed the Pontnewynydd arm (often referred to as the Snatchwood arm) of the canal, north of Pontymoile, and the associated 11 locks. Part of the line was later converted to a railway. In 1854 (and again in 1873) the canal was shortened at Newport to allow space for the developing railways to reach the docks.

Between 1850 and 1855 many tramroads were replaced with railways. The construction of the Blaenafon to Newport railway, via Pontypool removed significant trade from the Monmouthshire Canal.

The Brecon & Merthyr Tydfil Junction Railway was formed in 1858, building a line between Brecon and Dowlais in Merthyr which opened in 1863. The railway crossed the canal at White Hart Bridge in Talybont on Usk before starting the seven mile climb to Torpantau. The new railway followed much of the line of the Brinore Tramroad.

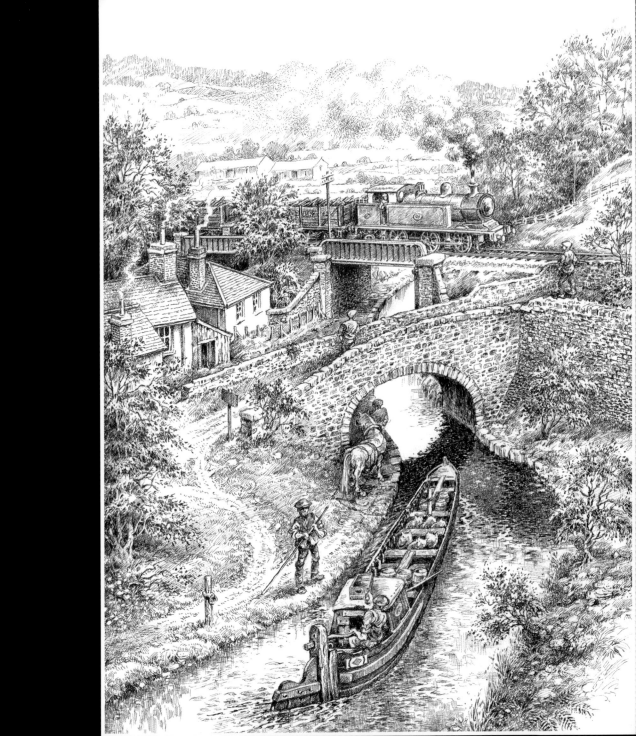

c1860

Govilon rail crossing

of the Merthyr, Tredegar and
Railway commenced in 1860 with
opening by Mrs. Crawshay Bailey
y. The railway was operating by
the canal at Govilon.

Brecknock & Abergavenny Canal
the Monmouthshire Railway and
y. Then in 1880 the Great Western
R) bought this business giving the
of both the Monmouthshire Canal

and the Brecknock & Abergavenny Canal with
their associated tram and railroads.

The Merthyr, Tredegar and Abergavenny Railway
was taken over by the London and North Western
Railway specifically to compete with the GWR.

Coal haulage, on the Merthyr, Tredegar and
Abergavenny Railway, peaked in 1917 when
5,000 tons of coal was carried daily from the
valleys to Scotland to fuel the British fleet.

c1908

Edwardian Sunday school outing

Boat outings became regular events especially during the 1890s and continued into the 1930s.

Working boats were cleaned out and up to 50 people were carried starting from various wharfs along the canal, notably: Brecon to Brynich Lock where they stopped to play sports, Talybont on Usk to Brynich, Llangynidr to Govilon and Llanfoist to Llangattock as pictured.

Increasing use of railways for freight transportation inevitably led to a decline in transportation by boat. By this time many other UK canals had adopted steam and diesel technology for their narrowboats, but the large number of locks and relatively short distances involved on the Monmouthshire and Brecknock & Abergavenny Canals meant that these conversions would have been less viable.

The construction of the double drawbridge at Cordes' Dos Nail Works Wharf enabled trains to deliver coal, rendering the wharf redundant.

c1915

The last canal tolls

1915 saw the end of regular commercial operations using the canal; railways now dominated the trade.

The last commercial cargo on the Brecknock & Abergavenny canal was one ton of lime from Llangynidr to Govilon, recorded on 22nd February 1933.

For the Crumlin Arm the last toll was for a boat load of furniture in 1935.

1938 saw the last toll on the Monmouthshire main line.

c1948

Nationalisation

In 1948 nationalisation of Britain's transport network meant that control of most of the UK's canals (now mainly owned by the railway companies) was transferred to the British Transport Commission. In 1953 the inland waterways were separated from the commission to form the British Transport Waterways which closed the Crumlin Arm in 1954 followed by the Monmouthshire main line from Newport to Pontymoile.

The Brecknock & Abergavenny Canal was saved from closure and remained in water due to industry at Pontypool which required large amounts of cooling water extracted from the canal. However, mounting maintenance costs forced local authorities to consider culverting many of the canal bridges. The Inland Waterways Association was instrumental in raising public awareness of these plans and sufficient interest was generated to force the local authority to reconsider.

In 1957 the Brecknock & Abergavenny Canal was included in the boundaries of the newly formed Brecon Beacons National Park, making it the only canal set almost entirely within a national park. Ironically, this did not prevent the top end of the canal basin being filled in during the redevelopment of Brecon in 1960.

It wasn't long before the railways, which quickly brought about the demise of the canals, were themselves under threat. Goods were increasingly being moved off the railways to roads as the rapid expansion of trunk roads enabled greater flexibility and speed.

Two major reports drove the final nails into the coffin of many of South Wales' railways: The Modernisation Plan of 1955 and Dr Richard Beeching's report "The Reshaping of British Railways" released in 1962. These saw the closure of the Merthyr, Tredegar & Abergavenny Railway and the Brecon & Merthyr Tydfil Junction Railway.

The last train to Merthyr left Abergavenny on the 5th January 1958.

c1960

Tourism

The summer of 1960 saw the first canal boat available for hire from J. R. & J. E. Tod at Gilwern Wharf, a 23ft by 7ft 6in wooden cruiser sleeping three. It was powered by an Austin 7 engine and cost £18 for a week, peak season. In 1962 larger centre cockpit cruisers were available sleeping five.

Initially the navigable section of the canal was limited from bridge 100 south of Gilwern to Llangynidr, as the locks were dilapidated, and the bridge too low to pass under. During 1962 the bottom gates of the first two locks were replaced with ones from the Monmouthshire section, while the others were newly built. By the summer of 1962 navigation had been restored from Pontymoile to Talybont on Usk.

1963 saw the formation of the British Waterways Board which took over the ownership of the canals and their associated structures from the British Transport Commission.

The Transport Act of 1968 gave canals a new future promoting their use for recreational purposes.

1970 was another milestone year seeing the restoration of the navigation to Brecon. This was accomplished by the replacement of the fixed road bridge at Talybont on Usk with a new steel drawbridge.

It is said that the original lift bridge had its lifting mechanism removed after a local councillor failed to notice the bridge was open and drove into the canal. The new steel drawbridge was initially winch operated by hand, but later converted to electric control.

c1984
A set back: Monmouthshire Canal partially filled

Despite the general trend of reopening canals throughout the UK, the Monmouthshire Canal suffered another setback when in 1984 the canal was filled-in between bridges 40 and 42 in Cwmbran. This allowed for the building of Cwmbran Drive, a new road linking the town centre to the A4042 and the construction of a retail park.

The vision and commitment of all those involved in its restoration have ensured that the Brecknock & Abergavenny Canal and parts of the Monmouthshire Canal are now a thriving waterway.

The canals are open to navigation from Five Locks in Cwmbran to Brecon, enabling pleasure boats to cruise 36 of the original 44 miles and navigate 6 locks.

Today the canals support six hire bases, three marinas and around 450 private pleasure boats.

The income the canal brings to the local economy from tourism spending is estimated at £17m per year. Additional benefits to the area include an uplift in property prices adjacent to the canal. Improvements in health and wellbeing as a result of boating, fishing, cycling and walking are now widely recognised.

2012

Full restoration

Full restoration of the canal both from Five Locks (Cwmbran) and from Crumlin to Newport is now underway, with the Monmouthshire, Brecon and Abergavenny Canals Trust leading the project.Grants have been awarded from numerous organisations including the Heritage Lottery Fund, Cadw, local authorities and landfill tax receipts.

Restoration is progressing enthusiastically led by the Trust's restoration team together with the Waterways Recovery Group and the local community.

Engineering studies have been commissioned to overcome many obstacles, including the road bridge at Five Locks, Cwmbran Drive and the low bridge at Two Locks just south of Cwmbran.

It is hoped that a small marina with associated housing and retail in addition to a sea lock will be constructed in Newport linking the canal marina to the river Usk and beyond.

Full restoration

Of the engineering studies produced, the largest project is the reopening of the closed section of canal at Cwmbran Drive. One solution put forward is to build two pairs of locks with a linking aqueduct.

Another is to construct Wales' answer to Scotland's Falkirk Wheel and have a trough lifted by replica steam hammers. The third less attractive option is to extend the canal around the back of the new development.

British Waterways is to move to charitable status during 2012 with the formation of the Canal & River Trust.

The future of Britain's canals will depend much more on the building of local partnerships and a volunteer workforce. The Canal & River Trust and Monmouthshire, Brecon and Abergavenny Canals Trust welcome interest from all sectors of the community.

ACKNOWLEDGEMENTS

Mike and Alasdair would like to thank the numerous people who were so generous with their time and knowledge during production of this book.

Special thanks go to Phil Hughes, Thomas Maloney and the Fourteen Lock Canal Centre, Richard Dommett MBE and Ray Haydon (Monmouthshire, Brecon and Abergavenny Canals Trust), John Norris (author of the Monmouthshire and Brecon Canal guide), Kevin Phillips (British Waterways), and Deborah Haylock (Haylock Consultancy) for proof reading.

BIBLIOGRAPHY

Chris Barber MBE   -   *Portraits of the Past (Blorenge Books 2001)*

D.D. & J.M. Gladwin   -   *The Canals of the Welsh Valleys (Oakwood Press 1991)*

John van Laun and The Brinore Tramroad Conservation Forum   -   *Walks and Rides along the Brinore Tramroad (Print Logic Ltd 2003)*

John Norris   -   *Monmouthshire and Brecon Canal (John Norris 2007)*

Gordon Rattenbury   -   *Tramroads of the Brecknock & Abergavenny Canal (Railway & Canal Historical Society 1980)*

R. Alan Stevens   -   *Brecknock & Abergavenny and Monmouthshire Canals (Goose and Son 1974)*

W.W. Tasker   -   *The Merthyr, Tredegar & Abergavenny Railway and branches (Oxford Publishing Company 1986)*

Ian L. Wright   -   *Canals in Wales (D. Bradford Barton 1977)*

BEACON PARK BOATS

Llanfoist Wharf is now the tranquil setting for Beacon Park Boats, a family-run business offering luxury narrowboat holidays on what is known today as the Monmouthshire and Brecon Canal. Owners Alasdair and Sarah Kirkpatrick run every aspect of their business from this private wharf just outside Abergavenny. In Beacon Park Boats they combine their love of design, craftsmanship, boating, engineering and hospitality to offer a fleet of bespoke 5-star canal boats and the superlative canal holiday experience.

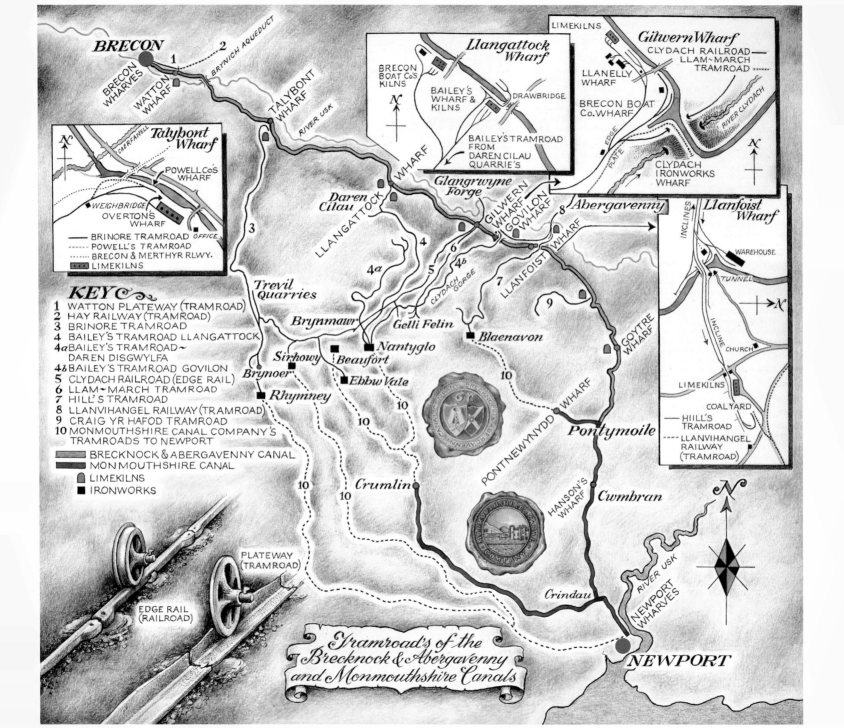

BRECON

BRECON WHARVES

WATTON WHARF

BRYNICH AQUEDUCT

TALYBONT WHARF

RIVER USK

CAERFANELL

Talybont Wharf

POWELL CoS WHARF

WEIGHBRIDGE

OVERTONS WHARF

OFFICE

BRINORE TRAMROAD
- - - POWELL'S TRAMROAD
······ BRECON & MERTHYR RLWY.
▪ LIMEKILNS

N

Llangattock Wharf

BRECON BOAT CoS KILNS

BAILEY'S WHARF & KILNS

DRAWBRIDGE

BAILEY'S TRAMROAD FROM DAREN CILAU QUARRIE'S

LIMEKILNS

Gilwern Wharf

CLYDACH RAILROAD ——
LLAM~MARCH TRAMROAD ·······

LLANELLY WHARF

BRECON BOAT Co. WHARF

RIVER CLYDACH

EDGE PLATE

CLYDACH IRONWORKS WHARF

N

Daren Cilau

LLANGATTOCK WHARF

Glangrwyne Forge

GILWERN WHARF

GOVILON WHARF

Abergavenny

LLANFOIST WHARF

Llanfoist Wharf

INCLINES

WAREHOUSE

TUNNEL

INCLINE

CHURCH

LIMEKILNS

COALYARD

HIILL'S TRAMROAD ——
LLANVIHANGEL RAILWAY (TRAMROAD) - - -

N

KEY
1 WATTON PLATEWAY (TRAMROAD)
2 HAY RAILWAY (TRAMROAD)
3 BRINORE TRAMROAD
4 BAILEY'S TRAMROAD LLANGATTOCK
4a BAILEY'S TRAMROAD~ DAREN DISGWYLFA
4b BAILEY'S TRAMROAD GOVILON
5 CLYDACH RAILWAY (EDGE RAIL)
6 LLAM~MARCH TRAMROAD
7 HILL'S TRAMROAD
8 LLANVIHANGEL RAILWAY (TRAMROAD)
9 CRAIG YR HAFOD TRAMROAD
10 MONMOUTHSHIRE CANAL COMPANY'S TRAMROADS TO NEWPORT

▬ BRECKNOCK & ABERGAVENNY CANAL
▬ MONMOUTHSHIRE CANAL
▮ LIMEKILNS
■ IRONWORKS

Trevil Quarries

Brynmawr

Gelli Felin

Sirhowy

Nantyglo

Beaufort

Brynoer

Ebbw Vale

Rhymney

Blaenavon

LLANFOIST WHARF

GOYTRE WHARF

PONTNEWYNYDD WHARF

Pontymoile

HANSON'S WHARF

Crumlin

Cwmbran

Crindau

RIVER USK

NEWPORT WHARVES

N

PLATEWAY (TRAMROAD)

EDGE RAIL (RAILROAD)

Tramroads of the Brecknock & Abergavenny and Monmouthshire Canals

NEWPORT